HOUSES WIT

Susan Utting

Two Rivers Press

By the same author:
Scratched Initials Corridor Press 1997
Something Small is Missing Smith/Doorstop Books 1999
Striptease Smith/Doorstop Books 2001

Acknowledgements
Thanks are due to the editors of the following publications
where some of these poems first appeared:
Daily Telegraph Arvon International Anthology
Mslexia
New Welsh Review
Pitshanger Prize Anthology
Second Light
Step Right Up
Ware Poetry Prizewinners' Anthology

First published in the UK in 2006 by
Two Rivers Press
35–39 London Street
Reading RG1 4PS
www.tworiverspress.com

Book and cover design by Sally Castle

Printed and bound by Conservatree
Print and Design Ltd, Reading

ISBN 1-901677-47-8
978-1-901677-47-8

Contents

Envoi

For Susie Green

I

We are all in the dumps,
For diamonds are trumps,
The kittens are gone to St. Paul's.
The babies are bit,
The moon's in a fit,
And the houses are built without walls.

TRADITIONAL NURSERY RHYME

Catechism

What is your Name?
Who gave you this Name?
What did your Godfathers and Godmothers then for you?

I come from a place with *beech* in its name;
my name then was wished for, dropped
from the mouth of an old woman, fat
as a grandmother, soft, round as an egg.

Conceived in the eye of a sad man,
I was born at the trip of a young woman's
foot, a tumble that rushed me, unready
to air, light, gravity's chill.

I was nourished on milk from the tip
of a spoon, sugar-sweet, thickened
with bread; and crucible tops from soft-
boiled eggs, made yellow, salty with butter.

I grew fat, white as a grub, gurgled,
babbled, spoke, settled for serious talk.
Loquacious, prodigious, I figured the world
in my mouth, made language a loose tooth

to push with my tongue – *cylinder, Hollander,*
colander, kiosk, – I rolled it around,
five years without stopping for breath.
I gorged on its sweet, salt, bitter, sour,

sucked hard on it, bloodied the roof
of my mouth with its acid. I come from
the quiet of a coy girl, dark-eyed, slim
at the waist, a girl in a green dress,

whose name then was chosen by men,
who taught her to lower her eyes, press
her lips, narrow her throat, swallow words
down; who taught me the power of *hush, hush, hush.*

My Mother's House

i My mother's house is full of birds and lodgers
sitting on the stairs, sleeping underneath the beds
and shinning up the drainpipes at the back;
she's downstairs, cooking on a disconnected stove,
with a cast-iron skillet full of earrings, small pearl
buttons lost from shirts, and silver collar studs.

My mother's wardrobe's full of ball-gowns,
sandwiches and biscuit barrels full of instant coffee,
there's granulated sugar in her dancing shoes
and corned beef in the pockets of her mother's mother's
musquash; she's counting out her trifle dishes, knitting needles,
crochet hooks, the motorcycle magazines and sixpences.

My mother's landing's full of women, queuing for the lodger –
the young one with the torch and cycle clips; she's looking for
an egg-and-bacon pie and a Thermos flask of tea to tide them over,
while the lodgers on the stairs begin a song her father sang,
with choruses, rude verses, all the twiddly bits and harmonies.
They're singing *Susie Green* to her, *we love you Susie Green,*

while she scoops vanilla ice-cream into amber sundae glasses,
adds angelica and violets, tiny roses made of marzipan
and coffee-flavoured biscuits, shaped like fans.

ii   They're in the garden – they've been there
every place she's lived as long as she remembers.
She remembers things from eighty years ago now,
better than from yesterday, ten minutes back
or that Scotch mist of time they call *just now.*

The birds are cleverer than clock time –
don't let them in, you'll never get them out,
flocks of them out there, beyond the window,
the ones you can't quite see, that no one else sees;

they're there disguised as dead leaves,
broken seedtrays, crocks and stones,
behind the weeds and bushes, in the uncut grass –
whatever tricks they pull they don't fool her,
she's canny, got their number, always spots them.

She double-locks the doors, keeps latches down,
seals off the windows, shoots the bolts at night.
She'd board the fireplace up, but lacks the know-how,
gave his tools away some time back now, or sold them,
can't be sure, is sure she couldn't have, she wouldn't.

And now there's no deep voice to shoo them back,
to clap his hands and curse, all night she hears them
shift and huddle, knows they're watching in the dark,
asleep out there, each one with one eye open.

iii He's there before her in the early morning kitchen:
    a stranger with a knowing grin, waiting, bold as ninepence,
    for her to switch the kettle on. He leans against the sink
    and watches, folds his arms and sighs, then tilts his head
    and waits for her to turn her back, to turn himself to air.

    Some days he's there again at dinner-time, never eats,
    moves his lips but never speaks; and when he brings
    the children – quiet little things with ringlets,
    button boots, old eyes in serious faces – she can't
    make out exactly what it is he wants of her.

    Lately he's been leaving things: old-fashioned chairs,
    fancy tables, unfamiliar knives and forks, stale cake
    and dusty ornaments – she used to find her way round
    with her eyes shut, till he turned up without a *by-your-leave,*
    grinning, giving her that look, as if he owned the place.

iv   All night she's dreamt of rowing boats, the heads of dogs
and flotsam bobbing down the street, bedraggled cats
with arched and shivering backs stuck high on rooftops.

She climbs a chair to look out of her window: not a sign
of paving stone or tarmac, the pillar box has gone, the shop
across the street starts two floors up with residential nets.

She watches shaky mirror-pictures in a dirty river, tries
to stare them still, to fix them there – *no nearer, higher,*
closer – loses to a kitchen stool that floats past on its side.

She climbs down to a dead phone, a double-bolted door,
no peephole to see out of, to see in through, a muffled
knocker and a disconnected bell. Upstairs, she's safe –

the only safe one left until they come, as come they will,
tramping higher, nearer, closer till they find her there.
She listens; then starts to drag the chair across the room

towards the door, the bolts, the lock, the handle,
imagining its stiffness, the creak of unused hinges,
the draught, the crack of light that might come in.

v   My mother's house is moving down the street:
it's a double-decker bus and she's on top,
she's looking down at Eric cracking jokes,
twinkling his gypsy eyes at the girls; and Phil
done up to the nines, Fred to her Ginger,
wowing the Palais crowd with his fishtail footwork,
scissor steps, and the double reverse spin-turn.

My mother's house is a travelling fair
on the lit-up common between the wars,
before the searchlights came and the lads
all went away; Mollie's there eating Five Boys
chocolate, dragging them back with her spoilsport
whining, scared of the switchback thrills
and the husky call of the helter-skelter man.

My mother's house is shooting the front door bolts,
putting up the towels: it's a snug bar round at the back
and Ron's calling out *last orders, time gents please!*
while she cashes up, turns the optics off,
pours a hefty double with ice and hitches herself
in her sparkly top, to the high red stool for one last
late night, all night lock-in session with the lads.

Her Bones

Her bones have leached themselves to honeycomb,
quiet and unbidden they have given themselves up.

While life was playing out its game of tag,
of kiss-chase, rock-a-bye, releasey-o,

its pantomime charade of chase-the-lady,
close your eyes and count up to a hundred,

ready or not, the witch's footsteps at her back
have sneaked up and have caught her out, unsteady.

While she's watched slips of moon grow fat
and slice themselves away to sickle blades

her bones have thinned to claypipe brittle
till she is a shepherd's crook, a rusty angle-poise,

a number seven; a three-legged hobbler,
story-book bent crone, blind but for the ground

to watch for specks and crumbs, a trail to lead her
back, soft-boned and snug, to where she started.

Sister

Underground, and the doors hum open, *please*
mind the gap and I do: I step out and I'm at the place
she went to when they said she was *too good to last,*
the place she offed it to, left me earthbound for,
where she fits in like an angel, living on fruit,
sweet milk and nursery rhymes.

        The scene is sepia soft-edged, musical:
out of her frame and mobile, fleshy now, she looks
the same as ever. She doesn't know me, so, for once
I have the better of her, think of playing dumb,
not letting on that I'm the one who followed her,
the one who lasted.

Today's Blue

Today's blue's nothing turquoise, it does not
shift in the light from duck-egg bright to aqua,
it is not a patch of sky to mend a sailor's trousers
or the uniform of girls let out in crocodiles, on pre-set
routes through Mellor's Park on Wednesday afternoons.

It's not indelible on children's tongues, or carbon
smudged on sweaty palms and touch-type fingertips,
nor is it jazzy/sad mood indigo for something small
you'll always miss but never really had; today's blue
is a memory of worsted cloth, tacked long and loose,

worn inside out, marked white with broken lines
of tailor's chalk. It is a man cross-legged on a table
in a backroom; it is not my father, though he's there
and with me and would understand the weft and warp,
the mesh of yarn, tight-woven to a blue so dark

you'd call it black; that he'd call *midnight*.

II

"All colours will agree in the dark"
Francis Bacon, Essays (1625)

Counting

Numbers are as definite as the blue
in my mind's eye that is seven,
as sixteen is always amber, shot
with the green of being four times four
and twice the perfect cherries of an eight.

And if sometimes a purple five is duller
than its neighbour, or towards a hundred
things get hazy, not quite beige or grey
but something in between, this is nothing
abstract. Just like the rock and tilt

of weekday stepping-stones towards
the concrete slabs of week-ends, like
someone's face you can't imagine,
quite, for being too far off: somewhere
in the concertina folds of memory
they're waiting to be coloured in.

Spanish for Love

It started with metal-tipped heel clicks, delicate toe-taps,
a rhythm that spread from her head to her footsteps on work-
morning pavements, then echoed on underground platforms

waiting for trains. Soon, she was snapping her fingers
in counterpoint, hearing guitars, intoning a melody
under her breath, castanetting loose change in her pocket.

As she waited at table, her skirts began swishing with
under-hem ruffles, gathered and basted in after-lunch
lulls, then machined into place on quiet nights in.

Weeks passed. She painted on lashes, blackened her hair;
months passed, she piled it high, slicked it back,
mantilla laced it, kiss-curled her cheeks and wrapped

her hips tight in the red sateen shawl, relished the flutter
and kick as it shifted, as it shimmied its fringes in time
to her whisper *Juanito, Juanito:* her Spanish for love.

The Colour-Blind Artist

i   The Artist

Sometimes, when he painted, he could hear red
in a minor key, distinct from green's harmonic fifth,
chromatic bleu marine or the interrupted cadence
of a yellow. And while his purples were less purple
than the everyday, he understood the tone of things,

the subtleties of shadow – to him the glare of others'
primaries were shades of the same thing, nuances of brown,
whole spectrums of it: buff to dun and beige, through ecru,
fawn to biscuit, sand and chocolate; and grey – he saw
the possibilities of grey, its fine distinctions, its infinity.

And when he loved, he saw his lover's eyes
as green, pale as the amber drops she wore,
as changeable as moonstones with dark centres –
dark enough to see himself in, clearly unrefracted.

ii His Lover

He wanted her with a flower between her teeth,
a poppy dropping pollen, black as her eyes' wide
pupils, as her undone hair – she'd be the gouached
star in his shifting sky. So she put on the gypsy
skirt and bit the poppy stem, held all his poses;

for him she dressed, undressed as goddess, devil,
clown, a blowzy barmaid, Faye Wray flailing her arms,
a still against a dated skyline. She was Carmen Miranda,
wish-bone cherries hooked on her ears, a cornucopia
tilted, jaunty on her head, one arm to steady it,

the other scooping her fluted petticoats, when
a trickle of purple grapes swung down and hid her eyes
from him, his gaze from hers. So he began to wind
her limbs with ivy, lay her down, piled lusher,
heavier fruit on her, then layer on layer of bracken,

stalks of yarrow, blackthorn branches thick with sloes
and finished with the rattling seedpod heads of poppies.

iii   His Studio

One morning she got there and found
his canvases turned to the walls,
all artifacts dust-sheeted over,
no furbelows, manacles, wigs,
disguises and costumes all gone;

just him in the snowdrift of linen,
her in her usual street clothes
damp from the trudge through the rain.

She was there in his eau-de-nil eyes,
as fingers eased buttons through loops,
pins released, hair loosened, fell,
a trickle of silk from her arms,
the soles of her feet on the floor.

For Herself

Today, she will buy tulips for herself, because
she's worth it; from a supermarket tub

of bright white blooms she'll choose her bunch:
tight-budded, sealed in cellophane that crackles

nicely, that will split like silk between
her kitchen scissors' blades. With her knife

she'll cut the stems by inches, at a slant
and clean – today she'll celebrate

the lack of shilly-shally buying tulips
for herself, the absence of *he-loves-me-*

loves-me-not about the petals folded
in their capsuled, green-tipped, calyxed heads.

And time will pass and she will watch for them
to open, convent-waxy, first-communion-frocked,

cool and smooth as the vase she'll choose for them,
white as the perfect walls they'll blend against.

But when they open they'll be shocking yellow, frilled
and fluted at the edges, they'll be vulgar skirted

chorus girls, and she'll laugh at herself, to herself
each time she passes, sees them opening their rude

mouths wider, wider still until they're flaunting
their sex at her, their dusty little bright-heart centres

and she'll throw back her head and laugh out loud
for buying tulips, tight white tulips, for herself.

Memorial

One day she'll plant a tree,
the sort with gaudy summer berries
and flouncy leaves that fall in winter.

She'll decorate its naked arms with scraps
of Spanish lace and lanterns made from
tissue paper, cotton thread and glue.

She'll paint its trunk snow-blizzard white,
(two careful coats) then take her pocket knife
to etch it with initials inside crossword grids.

She'll shower it with confetti made from
artists' cards from galleries, photographs
of long week-ends and holepunch polkadots.

She'll watch it from her window –
like the look of it, the way it nods
as if it knows her; the way it scatters

paper, lace and flakes of blizzard white
that will not melt like snow on warm earth,
                                snow on skin.

What Lasts

She'd often been beguiled by clever men,
quick-tongued and nimble-fingered, like
the paper-folding poet she'd encountered,
briefly, once.

          Another had the perfect mouth
to blow her smoke rings – she'd loved the way
he tipped his head back, chin up, neck stretched
taut, the way his throat moved with each puff
after puff of perfect circle in the air.

An early lover brought her winkles from the East
coast, wrapped in paper pokes; he sometimes
tossed her pancakes, fed her gingerbread,
and danced with her.

          A special favourite travelled far
by bus and train with all his own utensils, knives
and cooking pots to roast her aubergines, sweet
capsicum and artichokes.

Some brought her flowers – once, a quiet man
from Manchester came carrying a reclaimed
bishop's mitre chimney pot he'd planted
with geraniums.

          She liked the gesture – like the topiarist
who'd hidden in her garden night after night
until her box hedge slowly shaped itself to a row
of neat green hearts.

But she could not forget a Benedick who'd
matched her, wit for wit with a straight face,
who could toss grapes really high, catch them
in his teeth and feed them to her, mouth to mouth
without his lips quite touching hers.

To a Woman at the End of an Affair

Forget Delilah: remember all the lovers you will leave,
forget the few who will leave you, remember then
the smell of just washed hair, the squeak between
somebody else's fingers, the towel cape, clipped
at the front like a bunch of paid-off cheque stubs.

Feel the tug of the comb, the teasing through
to smooth, the cold curtain across your face,
the wait. There is a pleasure in the sound of sharp steel
cutting wet hair, like a guillotine through heavy paper
or your mother's pattern scissors cutting taffeta.

This is what we do: we close our eyes and dream a little,
wake and shake our shingled heads, our bobs and urchins,
smile and thank reflected faces, nod at our accomplices
and walk away relieved, of something; *light-headed*'s
not the word for it, exactly, simply there's a lightness

in our tread, a softening of shoulders, neck, our arms
swing easier, our naked foreheads smooth, our eyes –
remember this – each time, our eyes become a little clearer.

Fine

Then some days loss is tangible as the ice
you chip and claw at till your fingers numb,
go sticky and red. Or it's shrill

as the scream of a scalded child
that won't be hushed, hears its own voice
echo far off, make a sound like someone else.

Like a glass that's rinsed and polished back
to a glint, to ring at a finger's flick,
this is fine; as fine as the flutter

under the bone-cage place where
the muscle you once called heart is.

Let me count the ways:

i Follow the corkscrew climb, the steady drag
   foot after foot on triangles of worn stone
   till you're high as a factory chimney, packed
   with dynamite: breathe deep as you fall
   in black-and-white slow motion.

ii Speed-queen down the sliproad,
    zigzag over the fast lane, central
    reservation, jam the brakes, let go
    the wheel, spin, screech: not ice but fire.

iii Branded on one cheek, pockets full
     of stones and pennyweights:
     sink like an innocent witch.

iv Warm with wine and loving, drunk
    with a chemical glow, narcoticized
    to a flick-book story: play it back,
    again Sam, start to finish, then
    let the pages go, watch them flutter.

v The bone in my chest
   is a wishbone: wish for the snap
   of a quick rope.

Woodwork

I'm building a box: not quick-assembled
with an Allen key and diagram, not pine
or MDF or even beech veneer, this one
is patina'd and grained in walnut,
dovetailed, countersunk and bevelled,
heavy-lidded, hinged with solid brass.

It's big: just big enough to hold
New York, a pilgrimage to Northern Spain,
a framed collage of cheapday travel cards
to castles; and a house with elbow-room
for two, sky windows and the sound
of Chinese wind chimes telling tales.

The picture of a person lying
at a crossroads will fit in beside
the sound his body made as it hit metal
and the way it trembled, bled along
with all the promises the morning
had just made about its afternoon.

The lid and body marry perfectly,
a soft click as the catch slips
into place – no need for chains
or padlocks; tap its sides and listen,
clench your fist and knock to hear
its low-pitched, empty echo.

The Woman From Sark

What she missed was the sound of her own tongue,
that easy patois everyone knew, where everyone knew
who she was like the lapping of water, the look
of the sea, familiar and full in the eye as a friend,
cousin, kinswoman, relative, reconciled enemy.

That, and the clean mist, the soft-focus mizzle
that left her with salt on her skin and a fresh
damp in her bones to be warmed by the ashfire
of home, fed from a table she knew like the lines
on her mother's face, like her brother's voice.

Here there were streets to be wandered at night,
the echo of footfall on hard ground, permanent light
and air that grubbied her skin while she searched
for a river, a dark edge to watch for a flicker
of tidal shift, for a sign, for a voice she knew.

The Man Who Stole Balloons

What he loved was the noisy smudge
of their skins, the rub of yellow on blue,
their puckered knots in a bunch overheard
and the wind-tug cut of the string.

He remembered mercury dropped on a bench,
watching it move in its special way, wanting
to trap it, to take home its dull lustre,
its curved weight, its strange, round meniscus.

He dreamed of a field of dandelion clocks,
himself in the gondola cutting the guys,
the tilt and roar; then the perfect lift,
up and away, the infinite yellow and blue.

The Amazing Spinning Woman

I push against the air, a swimmer
without water, I am a caught fish
on a barbless hook

high above the mosaic floor
where chips of zigzag pattern
blur to watercolour pale

underneath an amber roof, cheek
by jowl with gilded cornice, jade
green arch and barley-sugar twist.

My head is tilted to an angle,
sharp against the soft curves
of the ceiling, and my hair

falls back – a fur of hair,
the brush of a fox
on the back of my neck.

I know the broidered garlands,
hand-stitched swags across my belly
quiver as my body stiffens;

I grit my teeth on metal,
tighten jaw and neck, a flick
to jerk the wire to start the push,

the slow-turn spin; hold on
and push against the air,
push harder, wider, faster,

till I'm flying, till
I am a sparkle-hoop
against a painted sky.

III

"Begin at the beginning," the King said, *gravely,*
"and go on till you come to the end: then stop."
            Lewis Carroll Alice's Adventures in Wonderland

Two Dreams

i Drizzle – steady, soaking stuff that blurs
everything; even my twenty-twenty eyes
are struggling to make out the shape
of a small horse – yes, it really is
a small white horse, dancing on the cliff
and clearly dancing salsa to a Cuban beat,
while a three-piece band of men in red bandannas
sways and sashays as they play a tune I know
but can't remember what it's called.

All I can do is stand there, tapping my feet
and watching, trying not to spoil it all
by shouting out *don't go so close,*
you're getting much too close –
you're too close to the edge.

ii   I'm trying to get to Italy:
you're there and out of reach, across
a waste of snow, drifted high as a man,
and I can't find my boots. Wearing slippers
I trudge and struggle till I'm hot with effort,
till my skin is burning and I'm wading,
then treading water.

                        It's like the time
we saw our daughter with her child, just born,
and we were there together, saw her beam
at what she held, at what she'd done.
You almost held me then, but I held back,
as if I knew the dream already, knew
how quickly body-heat melts snow.

Start at the Start

A summer, heavy with the thrill of being
just sixteen in a seaside town, with nothing
to spend but time, and nothing in between
you and all the beach hut boys with made-up
names and shady histories;

                              time to string along
with other girls who knew the ropes of looking
like they knew the ropes, who snapped the tips
off cigarettes for the cool kick, and licked
the thick shake taste of mocha from a tall glass.

Start at the start: a patch of grey in all those flash-
bright weeks, a friend who'd drawn the short straw
dragged you with her to a hospital, a friend of a friend
to duty visit, pass on classroom gossip, saucy cards
and Lucozade to.

                    I knew the words of the songs
from musicals for what they were, so never thought
some disenchanted afternoon, like that, I'd see a stranger,
hear his name and mine and recognize a look, a wicked
glint, a fatal fizz against the disinfectant blur.

Saying Yes

Not the night the girl in the nextdoor room
asked you in to unravel her knit-one from her
purl-one, pass-the-slip-stitch-over; and you did;

not on the long walk back in the early hours
past the railinged, angeled cemetery,
nor on the first tube out on the District line;

not on the top of a seventy-three to Butterwick,
not in the back of a cab, on a seat in the park,
or under the clock at Liverpool Street or Euston;

not in the Union Bar, in the queue round
the Albert Hall; not in the Albert Hall
or the SKR over hot grey milk with a dash

but sat on the kitchen step of a shared
bedsit, while Jenny slept, while the woodlice
curled, while Betty's manfriend snored.

Noise, Great West Road

We knew that it wasn't the wind,
but the sound of the underground train
coming up for the air, over the wall
at the end of our area yard.

We lived semi-basemented, coal-holed
and railinged, at home to the overhead
drumming of boots from a neighbour
gone Spanish for love;

                         we were snug,
huggermug with West Indian weddings,
chiropractors and washing-line underwear
thieves; with paraffin stoves that caught fire,

doorstep shit, corner-shop pregnancies,
men who turned out to be women, bottle-
fight pubs, one-armed bandits that flashed
to the smashing of glass while the landlord

kept serving, and we kept on hearing
the Underground whooshing, as windrush.

Snow, 3 April

A year before, it had been perfect sun,
a light breeze and a small crowd of friends
(more yours than mine) out on bail in a hired bus;
some family (more mine than yours) all hats
and handbags, a crazy vicar, a home-made cake
in the village hall, a knees-up afterwards and us

away from it all, leaving them revelling. Leaving
us to bed down in our basement, free to love
the scrimp and save of getting through to the end
of the week, each week, while the shillings ran out
and the candles burned down to a stub and a wick
in a cold hard pool on a kitchen plate, while we

clung for warmth, for dear life, to each other
watching the snow that sometimes falls in April.

Phone call from the North

There's cherry blossom,
solid houses, poplar trees,
the grit we're after.

Rain, Washway Road

Last night it rained and I thought of the year
we landed Up North, miles from the soft South
of an English village gone urban, gone empty
each day when the men left and the women & children
were boxed, home-countied, dormitoried.

And they'd said – it'll rain, it rains like nobody's
business, up there it's all damp, drizzle and bog,
gossip and tea, accents, inquisitive neighbours,
chimneys and weather. The year we arrived, June

sweltered, the earth shrivelled up, went crazy paved,
the lawn was grey dust and the tarmac treacled our shoes
like nobody's business, like rain had never been heard of,
never mind seen and the Washway Road was a joke.

Last night I remembered the smell of first rain, of dust
going wet to the swish of a pair of Lombardy trees,
the snapping of twigs, the lash on cracked panes
of the house with no gas, no kitchen to speak of,
no bell to the door, lead pipes and no heat.

I remembered the whoosh of the traffic down
Washway Road, the smell of wet earth and the look
of the ripples in puddles, after the splashes
of children in red rubber boots; that year we arrived

when the garden jungled, the house creaked,
the neighbours rallied and we watched the soil
turn loamy and black, rich, like somewhere we knew
from before, like here we were somewhere like home.

Noise, Delaunay's Road

Not lead shot sprayed from a gun against a wall
or rattling on a plate from a scoop of pigeon stew,
not dried peas spilling on the old cracked lino
of the backroom wash-house, unconverted scullery,

not hailstones on the windscreen of the pick-up van
we painted red from rusty blue, but gravel
on a bedroom window, early hours of Sunday,
because we haven't got a front door bell.

Because you haven't got, don't need, a key
because I'm always there; because tonight
I'm not up, ready with an ear, a body, with a finger
on the latch to let you in because I've fallen,

dreaming of disasters, to a fitful sleep, deep
enough to nightmare on through theatre whispers,
half-shouts, half-cut anger; but not through gravel
fistfuls at the window till I'm up and you are in

and I am taking down fine wedding china, gold-rimmed
white, from off the shelves in the backroom wash-house,
unconverted scullery, till the old cracked lino's covered
with a beach of jagged rocks and tiny china gravel chips.

Breaking Even

I bruise easily,
heal fast – it's a family thing,
this taut, thickening skin.

The Room

There was always something odd
                        about the hang of cloth
across the alcove, a feel of angles
                        not quite true,
corners sharper than they ought to be, and damp.

We did our best with it, shrugged off
                        the damp as condensation,
argued over the fall of light
                        on the nap of velvet
on a chair, chaise, sofa, the weft of a patterned rug.

We'd gather there and ritualize a life
                        of sorts, a through-route
room between rooms where,
                        try as we might,
the wine was not left long enough to breathe.

We held our breath in there,
                              kept faith against the chill
until the drip, drip, drip caught out
                              the lie of condensation
when the lights fizzed wet and dangerous and the ceiling

fell about our ears. We patched it up
                              but never got it back quite seamless
after the flood; then you began to fall
                              asleep there, drunk on anger,
fear and whisky, earlier and earlier, on the chair,

chaise, sofa – the deep red velvet one,
                              the one that never really was
maroon, whichever way you looked at it;
                              we left you to it, waiting
for the rug to dry, the pattern to ignite.

Phone call from a phone box on the East Coast

And I feel the chill
that comes straight from the Steppes to
the point where gulls swoop.

Phone call from America

There's an echo on
the line: your double, asking,
after mine's answered.

Macadamia nuts from Hawaii

You brought them back for
her, not me, after you came
back to me, not her.

Spoons

Sleeping together like spoons –
      that tired old image again,
like the cliché you always come back to,
      the platitude knee-jerk reaction.

It's the way the thing goes:
      when there's nothing
that hasn't been said
      there's nothing to say.

So it's quiet again, like it was
      at the start,
when the fit was exact,
      like a classic before it's a classic,

like that line from the old song
      the first time you heard it,
like coining a shiny new phrase
      and not knowing

this is the one that will stick,
      that you'll hear
yourself saying again and again
      and again...

Dancing

Through all the years of jive and shake,
between the smooch and cheek to cheek,
we never lost our rhythm, or quite forgot
the private language of our bodies' lead
and follow.
        As waltzes turned to tangos,
when the music rocked too loud, too rough
to keep up with, we kept on dancing, waiting
for what always came, the contact of familiar
hips, fingers, mouths: that last slow dance.

Phone call from Hong Kong

The rug in the lift
changes each day, you say, but
the music doesn't.

Go On to the End

You say it three times, turn round, and it's over –
here's no unravel of hard knots, no teasing of difficult
necklaces, pendant strings, chains of fine gold, no untangling
of hair, parcel string, rope; this is no slow unpicking of stitches
from hem, dart, tailor's tack, satin or tapestry; this is not easing
the threads from invisible mends, nor even a straightening of wire,
unkinking of cable or flex, and certainly no to and fro,
no side-to-side pull, no frugal unwinding, rewinding of wool.

This is the sharp cut of the scissors, the knife of the expert,
the topiary shears; or the flick of the small clever blade
of the instrument made for the job – the quick-unpick tool
thought up by a genius, pending its patent, pocket-size, handy
and simple to use, as simple as multiplication, easy as saying
three words three times over, easy as turning around.

Marks Left

There's the ghost of a watch on your wrist
next to the stitched gash left by a spike,
a prank in the park that went bloody – bloody
funny it missed, came out at the back of your
hand; there's the one I forgot, left by a knife
down your back, still there like a flat, white,
unfastened zip.

                    There's the smooth part
of my scalded arm and the dark place on the heel
of my hand – a splinter of flint left under the skin
after a childhood fall; and the mark that was there
when I took off the ring I never took off, that I still
have, that I don't want;
                    that I can't lose.

Legacy

I leave you the green silk dress that wasn't silk
but shivered like it was, slipped easy as an arm
around a neck for the last slow dance at a go-down
jazz club night; I leave you a chiffon scarf

and Chemistry, the chill of the attic room we chafed in,
the basements full of strangers-into-friends
and the fire that blazed in the last one, one September
to come home to, weary, punch-drunk, bundle-laden.

I leave you the strange enthusiastic neighbour,
expert in the ways of trains and traffic lights,
and the jazzman with no sense of rhythm, the lie
of perfect pitch, our syncopating spoons and bones.

I leave you a singer with too many words to the line,
who made them fit and mean between the wheeze of chords,
the thrill of sitting there not shouting *Judas* while
the others upped and left. I leave you poetry & jazz,

the angst of anger, bears & squirrels, the kitchen sink
of cinema, the grainy grey of subtitles, the books
we'd *really read* piled round the edge of the room,
that rug, those ankle-bruising chairs, the suck of wind

that slammed the door, that smashed the glass, the sound
as it shattered, fell, the pick of our bare feet through it.

And Then Stop

There always will have been
the rhythm of the falling rain,
dark eyes and green silk dresses,
bedspreads made of candlewick,
a certain bird with a broken wing,
small deaths and double-jointed
thumbs, bare feet on broken glass.

And after the party that went on
too long is all over, when the final
gatecrasher has gone and the last
train has really been missed,
there will still be a drunk, who sits
in the dark in a room below stairs,
unbudgeable, glassy-eyed, grinning.

Postscript

Sheltering in a Paris hotel, that short week-end
you smuggled me in a long black winter coat,
my hair scooped up in some sweet girlish gesture,
to try out one more *might have been*, a couple
of *if only*s and *what if*s,
                            we didn't know
that while we loved, protesters were at work
in public places, daubing red on monuments,
wrapping toilet paper round park railings,
bandaging the statues to a freeze-frame drama
with a cast of first-aid volunteers and mummies
striking attitudes.

Envoi

Grace

And I always thought: the very simplest words
Must be enough.
     BERTOLT BRECHT

Let us give thanks for rowan trees,
their cheeky summer berries, leaves
set in thirteens, their pliant trunks,
their swish and riffle.

Let us praise eyes in every colour,
painted fingers, kisscurls, skin,
an ancient woman's preen and pat,
her soft shoe shuffle.

Let us give thanks for moths and bats,
their swoop and cheep, the voices
of small girls;
                    for windows, fences,
weeds through cracks, cherry stones
in uncut grass, for thunder-flies.

Let us praise days of the week,
the fit of years, the usual tides
and moons, all starless nights,
grey days, the stars, the sun.

Let us give thanks for streetlights
and uncertainty, oh, let us now
give thanks with old BB:
let us praise doubt.

Notes

Reference is made to the following authors and works:

Catechism:
The Book of Common Prayer of The Church of England.

What Lasts:
William Shakespeare, *Much Ado About Nothing.*

Let me count the ways:
Elizabeth Barrett Browning, *Sonnets from the Portuguese. xliii*

Legacy:
John Osborne, *Look Back in Anger.*

Grace:
John Willett and Ralph Manheim with Erich Fried, Bertolt Brecht Poems 1913-1956: *In Praise of Doubt; And I Always Thought.*